# Contents

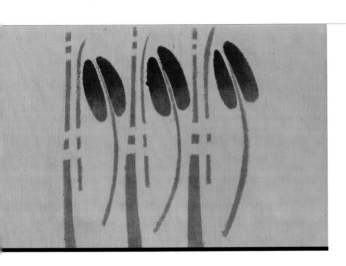

GLASGOW'S HIDDEN TREASURE
Charles Rennie Mackintosh's
Ingram Street Tearooms

# The Ingram Street Tearooms Project

Glasgow City Council owns a unique treasure – the interiors of the Ingram Street Tearooms. The famous Glasgow architect and designer Charles Rennie Mackintosh created them between 1900 and 1912, and they tell a fascinating story about his changing ideas on interior design. They are the only original set of Mackintosh tearoom interiors to survive.

The tearooms have had an eventful history since Glasgow Corporation bought 205–17 Ingram Street in 1950. Changes in the law meant that they could no longer be run as tearooms, and they became shops and stores. In 1971 a large hotel chain got planning permission to demolish the building and construct a new hotel on the site. Art historian Roger Billcliffe led a team that recorded the Mackintosh interiors before they were removed to a Corporation store. The team, which included Mackintosh's old firm of Honeyman and Keppie, made careful drawings, photographed the unfurnished rooms, and noted the position of each piece of panelling.

In 1978 the Corporation transferred the rooms to Glasgow Museums, and for 15 years they stayed in storage. Storing so many objects, many of them very large, presented special problems. It was difficult to find a building that combined enough space with suitable environmental conditions. Some timbers suffered damage from poor handling, fire and even the gnawing of rats. A Glasgow Museums legend tells of a cat found squashed flat between two pieces of panelling.

In 1993 work began on the restoration of the Ladies' Luncheon Room for an exhibition on the work of Charles Rennie Mackintosh. The exhibition in Glasgow in 1996 and its later tour of the USA were very successful, and stimulated interest in the rest of the rooms. Glasgow Museums has now restored the Chinese Room and the Cloister Room with funding from the Heritage Lottery Fund and Donald and Jeanne Kahn.

Left: Ingram Street today, looking towards the Gallery of Modern Art. 205–207 Ingram Street is the flat-roofed modern building on the left.

The process of reassembling, conserving and restoring
the rooms is like a huge three-dimensional jigsaw puzzle.
Some pieces of panelling, fittings and fixtures have been lost.
By the time the interiors were taken out of Ingram Street,
some rooms had been repainted many times, as you might
expect in a building used daily by the public. Working out what
these rooms originally looked like involved complex cleaning
and detective work. Other rooms were relatively untouched,
so that we can still appreciate their original finishes.

The rooms are a work of art, a testimony to Mackintosh's
ability to create beautiful and inspiring spaces. They are
also important in the history of interior design and the social
history of Glasgow. Research and conservation have already
revealed important information about Mackintosh's ideas –
the way he used visual effects to change perceptions of
a room's shape, his interest in unconventional materials,
and his experimentation with the play of colour and light.

For over 20 years the Ingram Street Tearooms have slumbered
in their store, a hidden masterpiece consisting of several
thousand numbered pieces of wood, doors, light fittings,
fireplaces and furniture. A team of Glasgow Museums staff
is now assessing what will be needed to research and preserve
the rooms for public display. It is an exciting project. We hope
it will lead us to greater insights into the creative genius who
was Charles Rennie Mackintosh.

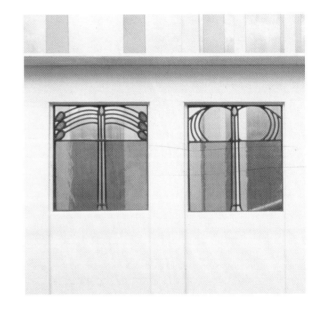

Left: Tea and scones in the Ladies' Luncheon Room.
Right: Leaded stained glass panels from the entrance screen
in the Ladies' Luncheon Room, 1900.

Portrait of the artist:
Charles Rennie Mackintosh aged about 25.

# Charles Rennie Mackintosh

Charles Rennie Mackintosh was born in 1868, the fourth of 11 children. His father, William Mackintosh, was a policeman of Irish descent, and his mother, Margaret Rennie, came from Ayr. Following Scottish tradition, his parents gave him his mother's maiden name as a middle name. He was born in a three-roomed tenement flat in Townhead near Glasgow Cathedral, the oldest part of the city. As his father rose through the ranks of the police service, the family moved to increasingly spacious accommodation. They eventually settled in Regent Park Square in Strathbungo, on the south side of Glasgow, where Mackintosh decorated his basement room with stencilling and Japanese prints.

Mackintosh was born with a twisted foot and always walked with a limp. As a schoolboy he had difficulties with reading and spelling, but his talents as a draughtsman were obvious from an early age. He attended Allan Glen's School, a private school specializing in practical training, and at 16 he started working for the architect John Hutchison. He enrolled as a part-time student at Glasgow School of Art, where he won several prizes. In 1890 he was awarded the Alexander 'Greek' Thomson travelling scholarship, and spent several months sketching in Italy. By this time he had finished his training with Hutchison and joined the firm of Honeyman and Keppie, one of Glasgow's largest architectural practices.

In 1891 Mackintosh began to give public lectures on subjects that included Scottish baronial architecture. He also turned his hand to watercolours and graphic design. Photographs show him as a striking young man in 'artistic' clothes – floppy tie, soft collar and tweed jacket. At this time he and his friend and fellow draughtsman James Herbert McNair met two sisters, Frances and Margaret Macdonald, and through them a group of women students who called themselves 'the Immortals'. With Mackintosh and McNair, the sisters became known as 'The Four'. Their art, inspired by the Symbolist movement and Celtic myth, evoked a twilight world of ethereal women and stylized natural shapes. Critics at the time called them 'the Spook School'. Frances and James married in 1899, followed by Margaret and Charles in 1900. They were a devoted couple and their artistic collaboration was to be long and close.

Right: Mackintosh and the Immortals, c.1893. Frances Macdonald is on the far left and Margaret Macdonald on the far right.

Below: The central light well of Martyrs' School.

Below right: Scotland Street School Museum, detail of exterior carving and window.

Unfortunately for Mackintosh, his firm worked mainly on alterations to existing buildings. He got his first major commission in 1893, designing an extension for the Glasgow Herald building with hints of the Scottish baronial style. In his spare time he turned his hand to furniture and posters. Two years later he designed Martyrs' School, to be built on the street in Townhead where he had been born.

The year 1896 was important for Mackintosh. With the Macdonald sisters, he exhibited at the Arts and Crafts Exhibition Society's show in London. He met the German architect and writer Hermann Muthesius, who became his greatest champion, and the tearoom proprietor Catherine (Kate) Cranston, who became his greatest patron. And he won a competition to design a new Glasgow School of Art,

although the formal credit went to Keppie as supervising partner. The Art School that you see today was designed and built in two phases, 1897–99 and 1907–09. The finished building is Mackintosh's masterpiece, the southern face towering above the city with its bold, clean lines. In 1903 he started work on his second commission for the School Board of Glasgow, Scotland Street School, on the south of the River Clyde in Kingston.

By the time the new School of Art opened Mackintosh had completed several other commissions, and his partners at last began to recognize his gifts. His first independent architectural project was Windyhill, a house in the Scottish vernacular style at Kilmacolm, built for William Davidson in 1901. The famous Hill House at Helensburgh, built for the publisher Walter Blackie between 1902 and 1904, was a grander version of this and reflects

Above: Entrance to Glasgow School of Art. The building's form
is enlivened by the tensions between plain areas of solid walls,
carefully placed windows and other decorative detail.

Mackintosh's extraordinary grasp of detail, not only in relation to design but also to the needs of family life. All the component parts had a role in the overall design, and furniture and fittings played an essential part in these decorative schemes. The same command of detail and brilliant use of light and space appear in his other commissions.

Between 1896 and 1917, Mackintosh, sometimes in collaboration with Macdonald, contributed to and designed an astonishing series of interiors for the redoubtable Kate Cranston. His contribution to Miss Cranston's Buchanan Street establishment was such a success that she commissioned him to work on several others, including Argyle Street, Ingram Street, the Willow Tearooms in Sauchiehall Street and her own house at Nitshill.

Above: Writing desk by Mackintosh for the drawing room of Hill House. Ebonised mahogany with luxurious detailing of mother-of-pearl, ivory, glass and ceramic inlay. Owned by Glasgow Museums and the National Trust for Scotland.

Left: Chair for the writing desk.

The Mackintoshes enjoyed a European reputation, exhibiting in Vienna, Turin, Moscow, Dresden, Budapest and Venice. The influential German writer Muthesius devoted an entire chapter to their work in his famous book, *Das Englische Haus* (*The English House*). However, despite their influence on other craftspeople and designers working in the Glasgow Style, general Glaswegian taste seemed to appreciate them less and work dried up. Mackintosh became depressed and drank heavily. He and Margaret left Glasgow just before World War I, settling first in Walberswick in Suffolk and later in Chelsea.

Mackintosh continued to design buildings and interiors, including 78 Derngate in Northampton for W J Bassett-Lowke, but he devoted much of the rest of his life to watercolours and textiles. In 1923 the Mackintoshes moved from London to the south of France, where he painted landscapes. In 1928 Mackintosh became ill. He and Margaret returned to London, where he was diagnosed as having cancer. He died in December, aged 60, and Margaret died five years later.

Mackintosh's death went largely unnoticed in his native city, although there was a memorial exhibition in the McLellan Galleries in 1933. Today he is acknowledged as a genius, a truly original artist and a figure of international importance. His contribution to modern architecture and design is now unquestioned. And in saving the Ingram Street Tearooms, the City of Glasgow preserved a major part of Mackintosh's work, which would otherwise have been lost forever.

Below: Domino clock designed by Mackintosh for W J Bassett-Lowke. Ebonised wood, ivory and plastic inlay.

Right: *Port Vendres, La Ville*, 1925–26. Over half Mackintosh's watercolours from his stay in France are of this subject. They reduce the small town and rolling landscape to flattened layers of angled planes, shapes and blocks of colour.

14

# Tearooms in Glasgow

Tearooms played an important role in the life of Glaswegians. They sustained office workers through the long day, revived middle-class ladies after the rigours of shopping and provided dry, warm meeting places for countless courting couples.

In the nineteenth century Glasgow had grown to become the industrial engineering centre of the world, the Second City of the British Empire. But it also had a reputation as a city of heavy drinking. Getting drunk on beer and whisky was an accepted part of daily life for many working men and women, and the resulting poverty, violence and disease were plain to see. The temperance movement that swept Europe at this time was at its strongest in Glasgow. A more fashionable and elegant way of combating drunkenness and alcoholism also originated here.

Late Victorian Glasgow rivalled London as a centre for the import and blending of tea and coffee. So it is not surprising that tearooms in Glasgow can be traced to the tea dealer, Stuart Cranston, brother of the famous Catherine. In 1875 he created a space in the sample room of his shop where up to 16 customers could drink tea on the premises, and the tearoom revolution took off. The Great Exhibition of 1888 in Glasgow encouraged the fashion. Nearly six million visitors enjoyed the novel pleasure of eating out in teahouses built in the exotic styles of the countries supplying the tea trade. The exhibition attracted business people, hoteliers and restaurateurs from France, Germany and Austria, and the fashion spread.

Tearooms took off as the city grew. Workers who had travelled into the city centre from the new suburbs needed somewhere to buy lunch. The city centre changed as women became part of the social profile of the city. Refreshment rooms were part of the late Victorian retailing revolution, as tearooms were established in department stores, complete with orchestras. Tearooms soon spread to the sites of other leisure activities such as roller-skating rinks and the new picture houses. After World War II there was a period of sad decline, until by 1975 it was difficult to take traditional afternoon tea anywhere in Glasgow. But there have been encouraging signs of a revival, and comfortable, well-designed tearooms are once again offering customers 'the brew that cheers but does not inebriate', although these days the brew in question is usually coffee.

Left: Argyle Street looking towards the Tron, c.1905, still a major shopping street today.

# Miss Catherine Cranston

Catherine Cranston ignored the conventions governing a middle-class woman's choice of occupation to pursue a career as a businesswoman. She took the concept of the tearoom and turned it into a revolutionary and very successful business. A champion of the 'Glasgow Style', and in particular Mackintosh, she created artistic tearooms that were unique to Glasgow. In her premises the public were able to immerse themselves in sophisticated, avant-garde interiors. In 1909, Miss Cranston made her first appearance in *Who's Who in Glasgow*, one of only five women to be included among the 461 entries, and the only businesswoman. Miss Cranston was an instantly recognizable figure, not least because she liked to wear dresses that were 30 years behind the times. In 1892 she married the businessman John Cochrane. He was eight years younger than she was and also dressed in his own distinctive style. His wedding present to her was a lease on a property in Argyle Street which she developed into a major tearoom.

Miss Cranston provided an excellent service for her customers, anticipating their every need. The architect Edwin Lutyens, one of her greatest admirers, left a description of Miss Cranston and her tearooms (see picture caption). The much-discussed artistic interior décor and her carefully cultivated image show that she was also very aware of the business value of what we now call presentation, marketing and brand recognition. Her tearooms had a certain distinction and commercial edge over the numerous rival establishments springing up across the city.

Below: Portrait of Miss Cranston by James Craig Annan, c. late 1890s: *a dark, busy, fat wee body with black sparky luminous eyes, wears a bonnet garnished with roses, and has made a fortune by supplying cheap foods in surroundings prompted by the New Art Glasgow School* (Edwin Lutyens).

Below: Menu card from Miss Cranston's White Cockade tearooms at the 1911 Scottish National Exhibition, Kelvingrove Park. Her customers could expect the highest quality food and service. A cup of tea cost 3d and a five-course meal 2/6d.

## :: Tea-Room Tariff ::

**Tea—**

| | | |
|---|---|---|
| CUP OF TEA, | Small, | 3d. |
| CUP OF TEA, | Large, | 4d. |
| RUSSIAN TEA, | Glass, | 3d. |
| POTS OF TEA (2 or 4 Cups), | Per Cup, | 3d. |

Melrose's " Queen's Tea " used, 3/2 per lb.

**Coffee, Cocoa, Chocolate—**

| | | |
|---|---|---|
| CUP OF COFFEE OR COCOA, | Small, | 3d. |
| CUP OF COFFEE OR COCOA, | Large, | 4d. |
| CUP OF CHOCOLATE AND WHIPPED CREAM, | | 4d. and 6d. |

Melrose's Coffee used, 2/- per lb.

**Milk—**

| | | |
|---|---|---|
| GLASS OF MILK, | | 2d. |
| GLASS OF MILK, HOT, | | 3d. |
| GLASS OF BUTTER MILK, | | 1½d. |

**Breads—**

| | | |
|---|---|---|
| BREAD, BUTTERED, | Per Slice, | 2d. |
| SCONES, BUTTERED, | Each, | 2d. |
| PANCAKES, BUTTERED OR JELLIED, | " | 2d. |
| PANCAKES OR SCONES, HOT, JELLIED, | " | 2d. |
| (Served for Afternoon Tea.) | | |
| POTATO SCONES, BUTTERED, | | 1d. |
| BREAD, SCONES, AND PANCAKES, Plain, | | 1d. |
| POT OF JAM, JELLY, OR MARMALADE, | | 1d. |

**Cakes—**

| | | |
|---|---|---|
| CAKES, All Varieties, | Each, | 2d. |
| BISCUITS, MIXED, in Special Packets, | " | 2d. |
| BISCUITS, Varied, Plain, | " | 1d. |
| BUNS, Varied, Plain, | " | 1d. |
| POT OF JAM, JELLY, OR MARMALADE, | " | 1d. |

**Sandwiches and Pies and Snacks—**

| | | |
|---|---|---|
| SANDWICHES, Varied, | Each, | 3d. |
| MUTTON PIES,-HOT, | " | 3d. |
| SNACK PIES, HOT, | " | 4d. |
| SAUSAGE AND CHIPS, | | 4d. |
| SAVOURY MEAT RISSOLE, TOMATO SAUCE, AND CHIPS, | | 4d. |
| MINCE, CURRIED OR PLAIN, | Small, | 6d. |

## Luncheons and High Teas

A la Carte or at Fixed Price. (See End.)

**Soups—**

| | | |
|---|---|---|
| CUP OF KIDNEY AND OTHER SOUPS AND CRUST, | | 3d. |
| BASIN OF KIDNEY AND OTHER SOUPS AND BREAD, | | 4d. |
| CUP OF CREAM SOUP AND CRUST, | | 4d. |
| BASIN OF CREAM SOUP AND BREAD, | | 6d. |

**Fish Dishes—**

| | | |
|---|---|---|
| FISH RISSOLE AND CHIPS, | | 4d. |
| POTTED HERRING, SALAD, AND POTATO, | | 4d. |
| FRIED WHITING OR HADDOCK, | | 9d. |
| FILLETED SOLE AND CHIPS, | Small, | 6d. |
| FRIED FILLETED SOLE AND PARSLEY SAUCE, | | 1/- |

### LUNCHEONS AND HIGH TEAS—Continued.

**Egg Dishes—**

| | | |
|---|---|---|
| POACHED EGG ON BUTTERED TOAST, | | 4d. |
| POACHED EGGS (2) ON BUTTERED TOAST, | | 6d. |
| SCRAMBLED EGGS ON BUTTERED TOAST, | | 6d. |
| SCRAMBLED EGG, FISH, AND RICE, | | 6d. |
| BACON AND EGG, | | 6d. |
| BACON AND EGGS (2), | | 10d. |
| SAUSAGE AND EGG, | | 6d. |
| SAUSAGES AND EGGS, | | 10d. |

**Cheese Dishes—**

| | | |
|---|---|---|
| WELSH RAREBIT, | | 4d. |
| WELSH RAREBIT AND POACHED EGG, | | 6d. |

**Hot Meats, Pies, and Savouries—**

| | | |
|---|---|---|
| MUTTON PIES, | Each, | 3d. |
| SAVOURY MEAT RISSOLE AND CHIPS, | " | 4d. |
| CHICKEN PATTIE, | " | 8d. |
| MINCE, PLAIN OR CURRIED, AND POTATO, | | 8d. |
| ROAST BEEF, VEGETABLE, & POTATO, | Small, | 8d. |
| Do., do., do., | Large, | 1/- |
| ROAST LAMB, GREEN PEAS, & POTATO, | Small, | 8d. |
| Do., do., do., | Large, | 1/2 |
| CHICKEN FRICASSEE AND HAM, | | 10d. |
| LAMB CUTLETS, PEAS, AND TOMATO SAUCE, | | 1/3 |
| MIXED GRILL AND POTATOES, | | 1/- |
| GRILLED STEAK AND POTATOES, | | 1/3 |

**Cold Viands—**

| | | |
|---|---|---|
| SANDWICHES, Varied, | | 3d. |
| POTTED MEAT, SALAD, AND POTATO, | | 4d. |
| ROAST BEEF, do., | Small, | 6d. |
| Do., do., | Large, | 1/- |
| ROAST LAMB, do., | Small, | 8d. |
| Do., do., | Large, | 1/- |
| PRESSED BEEF, do., | | 8d. and 1/- |
| ROAST CHICKEN AND HAM, POTATO, AND SALAD, | | 1/3 |

**Sweets, Hot—All Served with Cream—**

| | | |
|---|---|---|
| FRUIT TARTS, | | 6d. |
| STEAMED FRUIT PUDDING AND CUSTARD SAUCE, | | 6d. |
| CUSTARD PUDDING, | | 6d. |
| RICE CUSTARD PUDDING, WITH OR WITHOUT STEWED FRUIT, | | 6d. |
| PEACH TARTLET AND WHIPPED CREAM, | | 6d. |

**Sweets, Cold—All Served with Cream—**

| | | |
|---|---|---|
| CALF FOOT JELLY, | | 6d. |
| CURDS AND CREAM, | | 6d. |
| DEVONSHIRE JUNKET, | | 6d. |
| STEWED PRUNES, FIGS, | | 6d. |
| COMPOTE OF FRUITS, | | 6d. |
| SWISS TART, | | 6d. |
| PEACHES AND CLOTTED CREAM, | | 6d. |
| STEWED FRESH FRUITS IN SEASON AND CLOTTED CREAM, | | 6d. |
| TARTS, FRUITS IN SEASON, | | 6d. |

**Ices—**

| | | |
|---|---|---|
| VANILLA ICE CREAM, | | 6d. |
| VANILLA ICES, WITH FRUIT SYRUP, | | 6d. |
| VANILLA ICES, WITH SLICE PEACH, | | 6d. |
| ICED MERINGUES, | | 6d. |

Carson & Nicol, Ltd., Printers, Glasgow.

## Special Fixed Price Luncheons and Dinners
Served from 12 Daily in Saloons.

**2/6** FIVE COURSE, CONSISTING OF SOUP, FISH, ENTREE, JOINT, AND SWEET.

**2/-** FOUR COURSE, CONSISTING OF SOUP, FISH, ENTREE OR JOINT, AND SWEET.

(See separate Menu on Table.)

## Fixed Price High Teas
Served in Saloons at all Hours.

**9d. each.** CUP OF TEA, WITH POACHED EGG ON TOAST, OR WELSH RAREBIT, OR MUTTON PIE, OR COLD BAKED HERRING AND SALAD, SLICE BUTTERED BREAD AND A CAKE OR BUTTERED SCONE FROM STAND.

**1/- each.** CUP OF TEA (LARGE), WITH HAM AND EGG, OR SAUSAGE AND EGG, OR FILLETED SOLE AND CHIPS, SLICE BUTTERED BREAD AND A BUTTERED SCONE OR CAKE FROM STAND.

**1/6 each.** POT OF TEA, WITH BACON AND TWO EGGS, OR FILLETED FISH (LARGE) AND CHIPS, AND ANY THREE ARTICLES FROM BREAD STAND.

## Fixed Price Plain Teas
Served in Saloons at all Hours.

**6d.** CUP OF TEA, WITH SLICE BUTTERED BREAD AND CAKE.

**9d.** CUP OF TEA (LARGE), WITH SLICE BUTTERED BREAD, BUTTERED SCONE AND A CAKE.

**1/-** POT OF TEA, WITH SLICE BUTTERED BREAD, BUTTERED SCONE, AND TWO CAKES, WITH POT JAM.

## Suppers—Light Hot—Suppers
During Colder Evenings Served 8 to 10.

**9d. and 1/-** each for TWO COURSES.

(See separate Menu.)

**Drinks—**

| | | |
|---|---|---|
| SODA, LEMONADE, STONE GINGER, | | 3d. |
| GINGER ALE, | | 3d. |
| LEMON SQUASH, | | 4d. |
| LIME JUICE SQUASH, | | 4d. |
| SPARKLING KOLA, | | 4d. |
| MILK AND SODA, | | 4d. |
| CREAM AND SODA, | | 4d. |

E. 2000-13-2

Top: The Luncheon Room in the Buchanan Street Tearooms, c.1896, showing Mackintosh's stencilled frieze of monolithic rose-adorned ladies, entwined by sinewy organic tendrils and foliage.

Above: The Luncheon Room at the Argyle Street Tearooms, c.1898.

## Miss Cranston's Tearooms

Miss Cranston opened her first tearoom, the Crown Luncheon Rooms on Argyle Street, in 1878. On 16 September 1886 her Ingram Street tearoom opened, with a smoking room opening a week later. The premises occupied the ground floor of a warehouse and office block. Early newspaper advertisements show that businessmen were the main patrons. She soon bought the adjoining properties of 209–11 Ingram Street, and opened her next tearoom in 1888. She commissioned a fashionable decorating firm to decorate the room in the popular 'aesthetic' style.

## The Buchanan Street and Argyle Street Tearooms

Miss Cranston established new tearooms at Buchanan Street and Argyle Street in 1897 and 1898. Both were large establishments that occupied four floors of existing buildings. They show how Miss Cranston understood the business potential of creating tearooms with a distinctive and stylish environment. She employed the designer George Walton, who had designed interiors for her new home in Barrhead in 1893, to work on the Buchanan Street tearooms. He designed the furniture and some interior schemes, but Miss Cranston also brought in Mackintosh to produce some flamboyant stencilled murals. This was his first tearoom commission, and some aspects of his design were criticized in the press. At this time Mackintosh was a controversial figure, exhibiting with the rest of 'The Four' in the 'Spook School' style. Walton and Mackintosh worked together again at Argyle Street. This time Walton designed the interior schemes and Mackintosh the furniture. Mackintosh produced his first classic high-backed chair with an oval headrest to frame the occupier. In 1906 Mackintosh returned to Argyle Street to design the Dutch Kitchen, a basement conversion.

## The Willow Tearooms

Miss Cranston commissioned Mackintosh to design more tearooms for her ever-expanding business. In 1904 he completed the five floors and exterior conversion of the Willow Tearooms on Sauchiehall Street ('Sauchiehall' means 'street of willows' in Gaelic). The lavish Salon de Luxe of the Willow Tearooms is considered to be the pinnacle of his achievement in tearoom design and of his professional collaboration with his wife Margaret. In the Salon de Luxe the painted organic line of the Buchanan Street murals is replaced by the lines of the leaded glass and mirror that run around all four sides of the room. Drawing with this medium creates a unity of all four sides of the interior, because the design does not stop at the window frame, but continues across it. Today the Willow Tearooms are once again in use as a tearoom, bringing refreshment to workers, shoppers and visitors to the city.

Above: The Willow Tearooms 1903, stained glass doors to the Salon de Luxe. Owned by Blue and Green Holdings.

Right: Ground floor Luncheon Room at the Willow Tearooms. The use of white paint and the staircase screen with stained glass panels are a reworking of elements in his design for the Ladies' Luncheon Room at Ingram Street.

# The Ingram Street Tearooms

The Ingram Street Tearooms formed a complex warren of interconnecting spaces over three floors. There were two billiard rooms in the basement, a ladies' dressing room and toilets, a business ladies' rest room, corridors and six tearooms on the levels above.

As the sections on the individual rooms show, these interiors provide a striking demonstration of Mackintosh's stylistic development between 1900 and 1911. The rooms incorporate forms, motifs and design solutions from earlier interiors in both his domestic and public buildings. But these rooms also gave Mackintosh the opportunity to experiment with light and form, with new materials and spatial compositions that would reappear and influence his later work. These fittings, now in the care of Glasgow Museums, are the only examples of his many tearoom interiors to survive.

*Left: The May Queen*, centre panel, by Margaret Macdonald.

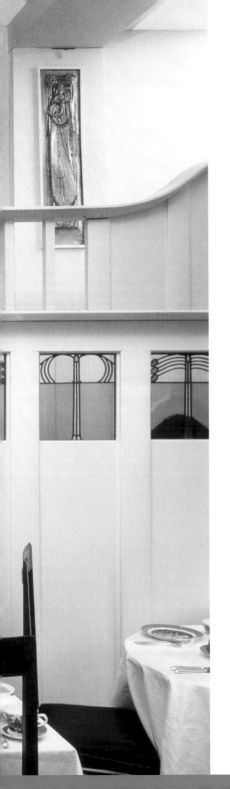

# The Ladies' Luncheon Room, 1900

Mackintosh's first designs for Ingram Street date to 1900, when Miss Cranston bought two shop spaces converted into one at 213–15 Ingram Street. Miss Cranston commissioned Mackintosh as sole designer, and the result was the creation of his first complete interior tearoom design. He transformed the ground floor of Miss Cranston's new acquisition into the Ladies' Luncheon Room.

The Ladies' Luncheon Room is finished in white lead paint and gives an impression of airy lightness. Mackintosh had just married Margaret Macdonald, and this room can be read as a celebration of their relationship. They collaborated for the first time to create decorative panels in gesso and beaten metal for the interior scheme. It echoes Mackintosh's contemporary white interiors for their new home at 120 Mains Street.

Mackintosh's design created not just a room but a complete experience, combining management of the architectural space with furniture design and a range of decorative features in a variety of materials, including stencilling, leaded stained glass, metalwork and gesso. His dark oak chairs, with their characteristic cut-out squares, provide a contrast to the pale colours and flowing lines of the rest of the décor.

Left: The restored Ladies' Luncheon Room, looking towards the east wall showing *The Wassail* gesso panel. The contrast between the noise and dirt of the smoke-blackened industrial city and this cool, white garden could hardly have been greater. Mackintosh designed a smaller tearoom above the Ladies' Luncheon Room on the mezzanine level, with direct access from the street front. A stencilled frieze of standard rose bushes decorates the walls to their full height.

## Restoring the Ladies' Luncheon Room, 1992–96

The Ladies' Luncheon Room played an important part in
Glasgow Museums' 1996 exhibition of Mackintosh's work.
The wood panelling of the room went through a rigorous
process of conservation and restoration to recreate the
original 1900 interior. The project team straightened
warped sections, repaired damage and replaced missing
pieces. They built a wooden frame to support the wall
panels. The windows in the north wall would have
opened onto Ingram Street, and this was the first wall
the team assembled. The south wall, which supported
and decorated the mezzanine tearoom above, was the
last section to be completed.

Analysis of the surviving material and examination of
photographs of the room provided information for the
restoration. The team replaced broken or missing glass
from the north wall, matching the stained glass carefully
to historic glass. Conservators cleaned all the metalwork,
such as the light fittings, to preserve the original finish.
The upholstery had long since gone, and the team matched
it with a dark brown striped horsehair. Modern replicas
were sourced for the table settings, and fittings such
as the vases and menu stands were specially made.

Right: Floor plan of the Ingram Street Tearooms as they would have been,
c.1912. (The upper part of the mezzanine lunch room and the ground
floor lunch room were designed by William Scott Morton of Edinburgh.)

Far right: The restored Ladies' Luncheon Room, looking down from the
balcony of the mezzanine. The screen on the right, with its alternating
stained glass panels of stylized trees, hides the entrance from Ingram Street.

**Mezzanine**
a  upper part of lunch room
b  upper part of Ladies' Luncheon Room
c  upper part of Oak Room
d  Oval Room, 1900–10

**Ground Floor**
a  tea room, 1886
    Chinese Room, 1911
b  lunch room, 1888
c  Ladies Luncheon Room, 1900
d  Oak Room, 1907
e  Cloister Room, 1911–12
f  ladies' rest room, 1909–10

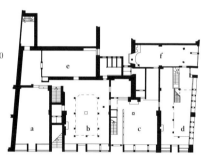

**Basement**
a  smoking room, 1886
b  smoking room, 1900
c  billiard room, 1900
d  billiard room, 1907
e  kitchen
f  storage

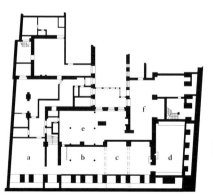

30 ft

15 m

Ingram Street

Miller Street

The Ladies' Luncheon Room, looking to the
west wall with *The May Queen* gesso panel.

*The Wassail* by Charles Rennie Mackintosh.

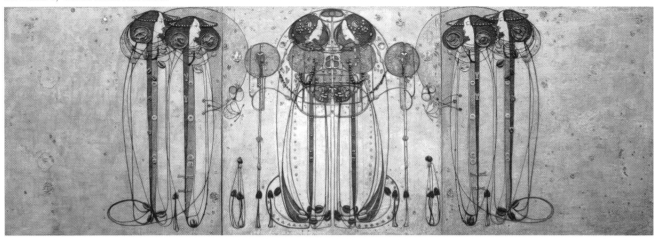

*The May Queen* by Margaret Macdonald.

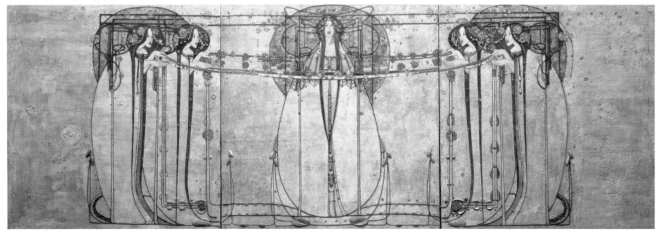

## The gesso panels: *The May Queen* and *The Wassail*

The focal points of the Ladies' Luncheon Room are the two large gesso panels, *The Wassail* by Mackintosh and *The May Queen* by Margaret Macdonald. They were mounted high up facing each other on the east and west walls. This was the couple's first experiment in this medium, and they worked together on the panels in the evenings. The titles of the panels may refer to two festivals in the pre-Christian calendar: May Day, heralding summer, and the wassailing of the harvest, ushering in winter. They first used these designs in 1899 in the sitting room at Dunglass Castle, the home of Margaret's parents.

These early panels are highly textured and quite crude. Gesso is a difficult medium to work in. The artist roughly applies the gesso, a fine plaster, on a loose-weave hessian, attaching string, beads and shaped plaster blocks to the surface to create the outlines of the figures and their decoration. Margaret refined her technique over the next three years, producing sophisticated, smooth-surfaced decorative panels with delicate lines, inset with tiny glass beads.

At some point in their history someone overpainted these panels with harshly coloured layers of emulsion paint, mimicking the original design. Once tests had determined the correct formula to use, a specialist paintings conservation team spent many hours of painstaking work bringing these panels back to their original condition.

Left: A conservator removing emulsion paint from the gesso panel of *The May Queen.*

Below: Serving table from the Ladies' Luncheon Room.

Left: *O ye, all ye that walk in Willow Wood,* Willow Tearooms, 1903. This is a later gesso panel by Margaret Macdonald Mackintosh.

# The Cloister Room

## The 1900 Cloister Room

In his first phase of work at Ingram Street Mackintosh designed his first version of the room that would later become the Cloister Room. This room itself may have been a redesign by Mackintosh of one of the very first rooms in the Ingram Street complex.

The room was at the back of the building on the ground floor, and in comparison with the Ladies' Luncheon Room was relatively plain. A contemporary photograph shows the tables laid out in regimented order. The walls are covered with canvas with a repeating stencilled pattern of a central stylized mayflower linked by repeating shapes of what may be either seeds or raindrops.

A glazed wooden screen flanks the entrance on the short side of the room. Above the height of the chair backs, it features a repeating pattern of hollowed-out stylized teardrops or tulips on stems. In the centre of each shape hangs a coloured glass bauble, catching the light like a dewdrop on a flower.

This early Cloister Room seems to be the only room in the complex that Mackintosh revisited. Perhaps this design did not stand the test of time, or perhaps it became just too dirty and worn, and the room needed a makeover to give the public something a little more avant-garde and daring.

Left: The first Cloister Room, c.1900, looking through the glazed screen towards the serving area and the waitresses' cabinets with their crockery and glassware.

Right: Mackintosh's chair for the 1900 Cloister Room. Dark stained oak with modern horsehair upholstery. Mackintosh also used this design in the Ladies' Luncheon Room.

## The 1911 Cloister Room

The last interior that Mackintosh worked on for Ingram Street was a redesign of the Cloister Room. Mackintosh reduced the room height by lowering the ceiling with a solid barrel-vaulted plaster ceiling. The ceiling is decorated with a low-relief rippling wave pattern. The walls are varnished wood panelling with a pattern like twisted ribbons in blue, green, red and off-white. This choice of colouring is almost identical to the successful colour scheme he had used in the Glasgow School of Art Library. At the rear of the room he placed asymmetrically arranged mirrored recesses. The mirrors are fronted by curved features that evoke traditional Islamic forms. They related for the first time to the organic art nouveau designs of the European continent rather than the elongated and flowing lines characteristic of Mackintosh's 'Glasgow Style'.

Far left: Detail of wall panelling from the 1911 Cloister Room, stepped out from the wall and decorated with a twisted ribbon pattern. Hat and coat hooks and an umbrella rack with a similar twisted pattern cater to patrons' needs in the damp Glasgow climate.

Left: Carved panel from the 1911 Cloister Room. Its lines seem out of place in the room, but its curves reflect the domed ceiling, and its wavy carved lines link with the carved and painted wave forms on the walls and ceiling.

## Restoring the Cloister Room, 1997–2002

The wall panels with the twisted ribbons of coloured lozenges presented the conservation team with a difficult decision about how far to take the restoration. In this room they were dealing with an original surface that had not been painted over, even though there were areas of damage and evidence of old restorations. The touching up or yellowing of the varnish had distorted the colours.

Only one domed section out of three in the original ceiling has survived. The team has kept it in its original condition for future reference and research. However, in order to recreate the original space of the room, a new ceiling was needed. The shapes of the ceiling were sculpted, and then a mould was created from which fibreglass and plaster casts were made. This recreated ceiling is made of a material called Jesmonite. Used with fibreglass, this material is lightweight but strong, durable and self-supporting.

Tests on the remaining original section suggested that the ceiling was coloured. The original dome was painted a similar shade of dark blue to the panelling in the Chinese Room, designed in the same year. We have no evidence for the treatment of the rest of the ceiling. The few surviving black and white photographs of the room are not helpful. We hope that further research will provide more information so that we can fully restore the original appearance of the room.

Above: The 1911 Cloister Room: the project team are lowering
the newly recreated sections of the barrel-vaulted ceiling into place.

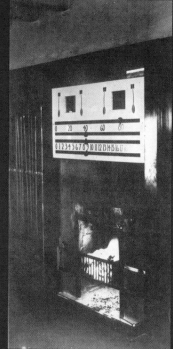

Above: The 1900 Billiards Room. Mackintosh's signature square shows in the legs and sides of the table and in the metal pendant lights.

Above right: Scoreboard and cue racks in the 1900 Billiards Room.

Right: Stencilled panel of stylized tulips from the 1900 Billiards Room, after cleaning and restoration.

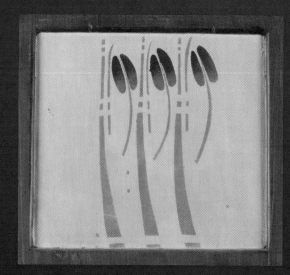

# The Billiards Rooms

Mackintosh designed two billiards rooms for Ingram Street. The increase in the number of office workers and the strong temperance movement in Glasgow meant that the city needed alcohol-free premises to cater for masculine tastes outside office hours. In the specially designed spaces offered by the tearooms the office hierarchy was abolished during lunch breaks and after hours. Here the bosses mixed with the junior clerks. It was common for billiards rooms and smoking rooms to be incorporated into these tearoom complexes.

At Ingram Street the male domain was in the basement. Here billiards rooms were located near the steamy heat of the kitchens, and next to the comfortable fug of the smoking room.

### The 1900 Billiards Room

The first billiards room at Ingram Street was designed in 1900. The customary raised and fitted seating along one wall gave the players somewhere to rest and watch the game, with a smoking area near the stairs. The ceiling was low with exposed timbers. The walls were lined with dark varnished wooden panels of a simple design. The top featured a stencilled motif of a repeating pattern of three tulips that line the room as if staking out the border of this masculine province.

### The 1907 Billiards Room

When the tearooms expanded in 1907 Mackintosh converted another basement area into a second Billiards Room.

The overall design is similar to that of the 1900 Billiards Room, with a low beamed ceiling and wooden panelling. One striking difference was the highly decorative carved centrepiece, recessed into the panelling on one of the shorter walls. The centrepiece was inlaid with cobalt blue glass and mirror panels.

Right: Detail of centrepiece from the 1907 Billiards Room. The carving suggests an ear of corn or a sprouting bulb. The personal and stylized motif of natural growth features in much of the early work of Mackintosh and 'The Four'.

Below: Drawing of the Oak Room from 1935, by Sir Hugh Casson.

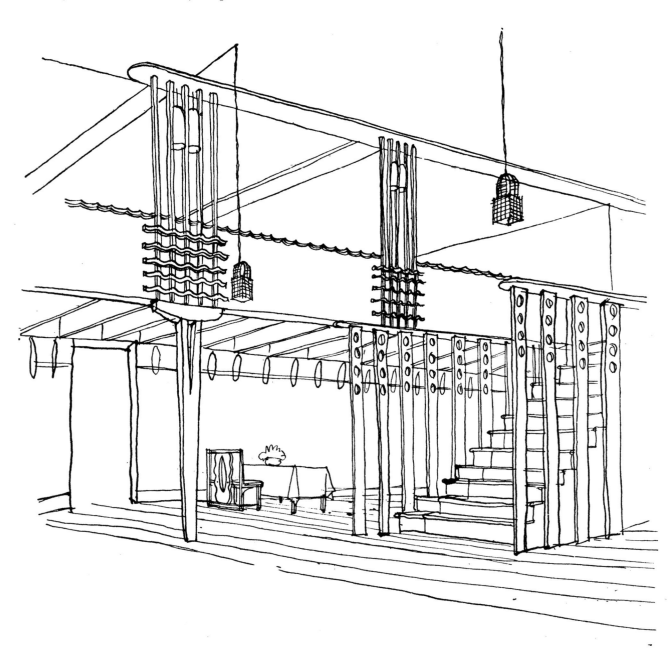

# The Oak Room

On the ground floor and mezzanine level above the 1907 Billiards Room Mackintosh designed the Oak Room, the largest of all the Ingram Street interiors.

The design is deceptively simple. Thick columns of oak topped by vertical lines of narrower wooden strips stretch to the full height of the ceiling. The delicate grid of wavy lines lightens their presence by breaking up the solid horizontal band of the mezzanine panelling.

Two walls of the Oak Room were external, and Mackintosh designed the space to maximize the amount of daylight entering the room. This raking daylight created strong contrasts, dense shadows and striking silhouettes.

The Oak Room's overall feel, with the mezzanine level balcony decorated by wavy lathe, echoes Mackintosh's contemporary design for the Glasgow School of Art Library, completed in 1909. In the Oak Room, as later in the Library, he unified the space by continuing the line of the balcony across all four walls of the room, even the window walls.

Although the panelling is made of real oak, it now has a fake wood grain finish, probably added in the 1940s.

Left: Dresser from the 1907 Oak Room. The wavy oak frills echo the undulating lathe Mackintosh used on the balcony, just as the line of cobalt blue glass squares reflects the use of blue glass shapes around the wooden panelling.

Below: Chair from the Oak Room. The wavy back and cut-out teardrop echo shapes that Mackintosh had used in the room's design.

# The Oval Room

The last area to be converted for public use in 1909–10 was a small space at the back of the Oak Room. It became two separate rooms on two levels, the Oval Room on the mezzanine, and the Ladies' Rest Room on the ground floor.

The Oval Room may have functioned as a small tearoom. The walls of the room were clad with a framework supporting canvas panels, converting the original rectangular shape into an oval.

The layout of the Oval Room is very similar to the Ladies' Rest Room below, with a bay window of textured glass flanked by three columns of mirrored glass that reflected light into what was otherwise a very dark space. This textured glass prevented the patrons from seeing out onto the 'middens' or dustbin area in the unsightly back court below. The design has features that compare with Mackintosh's 1904 music room interior for Miss Cranston's home. He reused his earlier design solution of using a slatted curved screen as room divider. This let in daylight and allowed customers to look down on the proceedings in the Oak Room below.

## True colours

The room panelling has been over-painted white. We need to carry out research to establish the original colour scheme and surface finishes.

Investigations to date have revealed that underneath the top layer of white paint lay an original dark wooden varnish finish, with finely carved relief squares highlighted in gold and silver leaf. We will carry out further tests on the canvas panelling, which now appears mushroom in colour. It is possible that there are stencilled designs on this otherwise plain panelling, as Mackintosh often stencilled wall coverings.

The colours that are starting to emerge from these investigations directly relate to the original colours in the Ladies' Rest Room below. There, dark-stained panelling flanked the windows and the small squares of gold appeared in the form of a gold mosaic-fronted fireplace. Further tests will reveal more about how the designs of the two rooms relate to each other.

Left: The Oval Room wooden panels, carved in low relief, from before *(left)* and after *(right)* restoration. The panel on the right shows the original dark varnish finish with square highlights in silver and gold leaf.

Below: Ink and watercolour drawing of Mackintosh's designs for two writing desks for the Ladies' Rest Room. Glasgow cabinetmaker Francis Smith made two of the one-person desks and one of the larger circular desks, accommodating four people, with its decorative privacy screen and stationery slots.

# The Ladies' Rest Room

The Ladies' Rest Room in the Ingram Street Tearooms was a new development, reflecting a growing acceptance of the changing status of women in society at that time. Miss Cranston had already provided Rest Rooms for men and Ladies' Rooms for women in her other tearoom complexes. This new room was to function as a space where ladies could conduct meetings or as a refuge between engagements. Later there were writing desks alongside telephones, telegraph machines and newspapers.

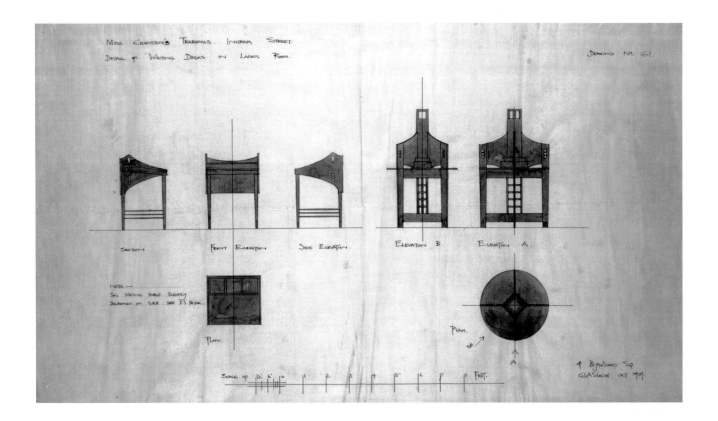

Right: Jessie M King designed a series of menu cards for Miss Cranston around 1917. The back of the card lists all the modern facilities Miss Cranston provided, including the Rest Room for business ladies at Ingram Street.

NOTE·TO·VISITORS

MISS·CRANSTON
PROVIDES·AT·ALL·
HER·PLACES·
SMOKING ···AND
REST·ROOMS·
FOR·THE·VSE·OF·HER
PATRONS·WHO·ARE·
ASKED·TO·TAKE·FVLL
ADVANTAGE·OF·THE·
FACILITIES·THEY·OFFER
FOR·MEETING·BUSINESS
FRIENDS·OR·RESTING
BETWEEN·BUSINESS·
···ENGAGEMENTS···

TELEPHONES·WRITING
DESKS·LATEST·NEWS
TELEGRAMS·NEWSPAPERS
DAILY·AND·WEEKLY·
BILLIARD'S·CHESS·
DRAVGHTS

AT·INGRAM·STREET·ADDRESS
A·SPECIAL·REST·ROOM·FOR
BVSINESS·LADIES·IS·PROVIDED·

MISS·CRANSTON'S
LVNCH·AND·TEA·
ROOMS
114·ARGYLE·STREET
91·BVCHANAN·STREET
205·INGRAM·STREET
217·SAVCHIEHALL·STREET
GLASGOW

# The Chinese Room

Mackintosh designed two tearoom interiors for Miss Cranston's pavilion in the 1911 Scottish National Exhibition in Glasgow. Later that year he returned to undertake two final schemes at Ingram Street. The first was the Chinese Room.

This room marks a distinct stylistic break from Mackintosh's earlier work. Both his 1911 interiors are darker, experimenting with repetitive geometric patterns, the mathematical manipulation of space, saturated colour, and the effect of electric light on reflective surfaces.

The design of the Chinese Room is dominated by the square. The room is painted blue, latticed and mirrored, with a pagoda-style motif echoing through its light fittings, cash desk and furniture. In this room Mackintosh displayed exotic influences, creating an enclosed interior that invites privacy, with lowered ceiling and subdivisions arranged like the screens in Japanese houses.

This room is less dependent on daylight than the other large rooms in Ingram Street. The presence of leaded mirror panels on three of the four walls of this room, combined with the effect of 20 pierced hanging copper lampshades, means light and the movement of light are reflected around the room.

Right: Restored furniture from the Chinese Room: two chairs, a domino table and a pendant light fitting with pierced painted copper shade and wooden pagoda top.

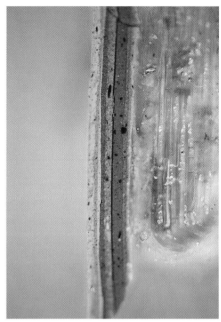

Above: The Chinese Room in 1950, looking towards the cash desk and beyond it to the entrance and windows on Ingram Street. Mackintosh's workbooks for the design and construction phase refer to this as the Blue Room.

Mackintosh was also experimenting with new materials such as casein, an early milk-based form of plastic, and the use of woven rush to create texture on the walls. The ideas in this room pre-empt the decorative devices and forms that appear in Mackintosh's later interiors, such as his remodelling and design of the terraced house at 78 Derngate in Northampton for the engineer WJ Bassett-Lowke in 1916–17.

## Colour

The Chinese Room has been repainted various shades of blue over the years, from a dark navy to a bright turquoise. To find out the original colour of the room, the conservator took cross-sections from painted and cleaned sample areas of the wood panelling. This revealed that the first paint layer after the undercoat is Prussian blue, and the room was repainted with a matching colour. The paint used in the final restoration of the room is lead-based. When applied with a brush this achieves a finish very similar in texture and reflective quality to the original paint layer.

Leaving the layers of paint untouched and painting over them preserves important evidence for the future.

Above right: Cross-section of paint samples from the Chinese Room. This magnified close-up shows the many layers and shades of paint applied over the years. The golden colour is the wood itself.

## What is conservation?

Conservators play an important role in museums. It is their job to ensure that the objects in the collection will survive into the future. Sometimes this involves active treatment to reverse corrosion or decay, but more often it means stabilizing original materials so that they will not deteriorate further. This is often a question of ensuring that the object is kept in the right conditions.

A team of specialist conservators have been using both restoration and conservation techniques to rebuild the tearooms. Restoration includes replacing lost pieces or treating original materials so they look 'as new'. Conservation is more concerned with preserving the original object as it is. Before carrying out treatment on any piece of the tearooms a conservator will research and investigate the best way to proceed.

With 'objects' as large and complex as a room, this is a complicated process. The challenge for the team is to bring the rooms back to a state in which Mackintosh's design can be fully appreciated by visitors, while preserving original materials and their importance as historical objects. The rooms are the 'canvas' of Mackintosh's design ideas. In order to restore these designs the team has sometimes had to repaint structures, clean away later paint layers, add supports and new pieces and remove small items such as rusty nails or screws. In doing so we could remove some of the historical evidence, and if we do not do it carefully we could reduce the authenticity of the rooms.

When we carry out this practical work we have to keep careful records of all research and investigation, including treatment options, the reasons for decisions and the type of treatment carried out. We use reports and photographs to create an archive of all our work that can be consulted in the future. On a project of this scale all the work is time-consuming and painstaking. It ranges from working out how to make a support structure from which to hang the room panels to taking cross-sections of paint. We analyse the cross-sections to identify the original colour and find the right mixture of solvents to remove later layers. Work to date has revealed more details of the designs we already knew about, and has begun to reveal new and exciting aspects we were not aware of.

In working on the tearooms the conservation team has used tried and tested conservation techniques. They have also developed unique methods and techniques in response to Mackintosh's innovative use of materials. With more rooms yet to be worked on we still have a long way to go to discover and restore Mackintosh's designs.

Right: Conserving the mirrored glass panels.

Right: Restoration work in progress, 2002. The Cloister Room is on the left and the Chinese Room on the right.

Far right: Beginning work on the Chinese Room. Putting together the four walls combines precision geometry and heavy labour.

## Restoring the Chinese Room, 1997–2002

The project team discovered through extensive testing and research that the plant fibre used on some of the screens is a type of sea grass similar to that used in Japanese *tatami* mats. All the original rush has been carefully cleaned to remove any loose and flaking paint. The team has repaired torn areas using Japanese paper glued to the back for structural support and newly woven sea grass sections at the front to recreate the texture. The few missing areas of sea grass were rewoven.

Because of changes in the way mirrors are made, the original glass panels would have offered a softer reflection than modern mirrors. Much of the glass has been damaged and the protective paint and mirroring on the back of the glass has corroded. The main conservation challenge with the mirrors has been to preserve as much of the original glass as possible, and the team has developed methods of restoring the silvering without otherwise changing the panels. We have replaced glass that has been extensively damaged or is missing with mirrored glass that is sympathetic in texture and tone to the original.

Right: Work in progress on the Chinese Room. The original wall panelling is hung on wooden support structures.

# More Discoveries to be Made

The customers of the tearooms needed private spaces for washing off the city grime and grooming themselves. Mackintosh took the opportunity to decorate these small but important spaces. Designed from 1900 onwards, the walls of the toilets, cloakrooms and Ladies' Dressing Room were clad in simple wood panelling. Decorative features are practical: a mirror frame and two towel rails are inset with vivid blue glass, and a shelf is decorated with metal cut-outs.

All these private rooms were entered through strikingly decorated doors. They seem to follow a colour code. For men, the doors are stained brown and inset with two vertical lines of squares of electric deep blue glass, and for ladies the doors are white with a single line of paler blue glass squares. There are many other doors, some more complicated, some simpler. Like many other areas of the tearooms, including the mirror shown here, most are hiding their true colours under abundant layers of paint.

Right: Full-length mirror from the Ladies' Dressing Room designed by Mackintosh in 1900. The project team originally thought that the mirror was painted white, but tests showed that its original finish was oak stained with green.

Far right: What the well-dressed ladies of Glasgow wore. Afternoon dress from Fraser & Sons Ltd. Matching bodice and skirt in petrol-blue silk with cream lace and embroidered panels, 1905–08.

# The End of an Era

After he moved south in 1913 Mackintosh never returned to Glasgow. He designed the Dug-Out at the Willow Tearooms in 1917 for Miss Cranston, but the plans were submitted on his behalf and he did not oversee the project. In the same year Miss Cranston's husband died. Devastated by grief, she began to sell off her tearooms: first Buchanan Street, then Argyle Street in 1918, and finally the Willow Tearooms the following year. Only the Ingram Street Tearooms remained under her regime, until she passed them on as a gift to her senior manageress, Miss Drummond. Kate Cranston died in 1934 leaving an estate of £67,476, almost two-thirds of which she donated to the poor of Glasgow.

### 1930 onwards: Ingram Street after Miss Cranston
Tea merchants Cooper's & Co bought the Ingram Street Tearooms in 1930 and ran them as 'The Ingram'. They made some alterations. Panelling and fittings were removed or moved around, and the tearooms boasted the fashionable addition of a quick lunch counter. In 1950 Glasgow Corporation bought the tearooms and the surviving furniture and fittings for £23,000.

# Some of Mackintosh's Work In and Around Glasgow

Two of Glasgow City Council's museums are housed in Charles Rennie Mackintosh buildings, and the McLellan Galleries display highlights of Glasgow Museums' internationally important Glasgow Style collection, including objects and paintings by Mackintosh alongside works by his contemporaries.

### The Glasgow 1900 Gallery
McLellan Galleries
Glasgow Museums
270 Sauchiehall Street
Glasgow G2 3EH (until Nov 2005)

### Scotland Street School Museum
Glasgow Museums
225 Scotland Street
Glasgow G5 8QB
Mackintosh's last major commission in Glasgow, now a museum of education.

### Martyrs' School
Glasgow Museums
Parson Street
Glasgow G4 0PX
A hidden architectural gem, one of Mackintosh's earliest buildings. It is currently used by Glasgow Museums staff. Open to the public by appointment.

### Ruchill Church Hall
17 Shakespeare Street
Glasgow G20 9PT
Two halls and two committee rooms, still in use by the congregation.

### Queen's Cross Church
870 Garscube Road
Glasgow G20 7EL
Headquarters of the Charles Rennie Mackintosh Society, the only church designed by Mackintosh ever to be built. Highlights include stained glass and relief carving.

### The Mackintosh House
Hunterian Art Gallery
University of Glasgow
Hillhead Street
Glasgow G12 8QQ
Mackintosh-designed interiors from 6 Florentine Terrace, Glasgow, where Mackintosh and Margaret Macdonald lived between 1908 and 1914.

### Glasgow School of Art
167 Renfrew Street
Glasgow G3 6RQ
Tours of Mackintosh's architectural masterpiece last approximately one hour.

### The Willow Tearooms
217 Sauchiehall Street
Glasgow G2 3EX
Mackintosh created the façade of 217 Sauchiehall Street as the frontage for Miss Cranston's tearoom. Step back in time to take tea or a light meal in the Willow Tearooms Room de Luxe and the Gallery.

### The Lighthouse
11 Mitchell Lane
Glasgow G1 3NU
Formerly the offices of the *Glasgow Herald* newspaper, now the Mackintosh Interpretation Centre, with interactive displays and architectural models. The extension to this building was Mackintosh's first big commission, and his tower provides magnificent views.

### The Hill House
Upper Colquhoun Street
Helensburgh G84 9A
Now in the care of the National Trust for Scotland. Restored original furniture, fittings and interior designs.